Mission Possible

"Spiritual Covering"

Believing for your Husband's Salvation

D. L. McCarragher

Alabaster Box Publishing Inc.

MISSION POSSIBLE -
Spiritual Covering
D.L. McCarragher

Unless otherwise noted, all Scripture
quotations are from the Holy Bible,
New King James Version, Copyright 1982
by Thomas Nelson, Inc.

Published by:
ALABASTER BOX PUBLISHING INC.
www.AlabasterBoxPublishing.com
Email: deb@alabasterboxpublishing.com

Printed by: Brentwood Christian Press
www.BrentwoodBooks.com

Revised Edition 2009
Library of Congress Reg. Number: TX0006839312
ISBN-13 978-0-615-30357-4

Dedication

"Thanks be to God for His indescribable gift!"
(II Corinthians 9:15)
To **JESUS**, my *Rock and Salvation* ...
my *Hope and Strength*.

To my **eternal best friend**, sister in Christ,
and mentor, Karen – who encourages my
heart, challenges my faith,
and covers me in continual prayer....
I love you more than words can convey.
"A friend loveth at all times." (Proverbs 17:17)

To my dear mother, Virginia,
who sees the fruit of her labor of tears and
prayer, that she might see Jesus in me...
"Weeping may endure for a night,
But joy comes in the morning." (Psalm 30:5)

To the *Power of Prayer,* the *Privilege of Prayer,*
and the *Promise of Prayer*
as revealed to me through
Unveiled Prayer Ministries
"Pray without ceasing."
(I Thessalonians 5:17)

Your Husband - My gift to you

Daughter of Mine, come close
and listen to Me.
I chose you first.
My strength is made perfect in your weakness.
Your husband is my workmanship. I have
ordained this marriage.
It is a divine joining
- a partnership
"till death do you part".

My grace is sufficient for you.
Do not take offense.
His actions are not governed by My spirit.
He does not yet know Me as you do.
You are the apple of My eye;
it is my good pleasure
to give you the desires of your heart.
That would be your husband - would it not?

Your obedience to Me and your humbleness
in the face of heartbreak are your sacrificial
offering to Me - one in which I treasure.
I am your husband now, for awhile. Let me comfort
and love you.

Daughter, take heart. You are not forgotten.
Can you see him? I am creating in him a new man;
in My likeness. Be patient... Trust Me... Wait.

"For the unbelieving husband is sanctified by the wife..."
"For how do you know, O wife, whether you will save your
husband?" (I Corinthians 7: 14, 16)

The Author April 1998

CONTENTS

ACKNOWLEDGMENTS

If your husband is unsaved, take heart. A man is most likely to be led to faith in Christ by their believing wife. The sacred Scriptures are not silent concerning your role as a believing wife with your unsaved husband. Deborah, has in *"Mission Possible"*, expounded scriptures to encourage women to believe God with a "radical" faith for the salvation of their spouse. She helps women fulfill their role in the marriage for the salvation of their mate. Give *"Mission Possible"* to any lady praying for the salvation of her husband.

In Jesus,
Scott Yirka, Pastor/Teacher
Hibernia Baptist Church
Green Cove Springs, FL

Mission Possible is written to reflect the complete trust in God for the home and family. It is the reflection of faith, patience and hope firmly rooted in God's promises. It is a reminder of Abraham's faith when "he called those things which be not as though they were."

The author has captured the meaning of faith over circumstance. It is illustrated by Abraham, who: "staggered not at the promises of God through unbelief, but was strong in faith, giving glory to God, and being fully persuaded that, what He had promised He was able to perform" (Romans 4:20-21).

She applies her faith and commitment to Christ by being a faithful member of the church and unselfishly serving others. This book reflects her undying love for Christ and devotion to her family and the ministry to which she is called.

This book will encourage others to believe for the salvation of their household. It will inspire the reader to believe that our wonderful Lord will honor the quest of faith in all pursuits of life.

Cecil Wiggins, Senior Pastor
Evangel Temple Assembly of God
Jacksonville, FL

"Mission Possible" lays out the battle plan for every godly wife to follow to impact her unsaved husband for Christ. Scripture reminds us repeatedly that a spiritual battle is taking place around us for the souls of our mates. Every faithful wife must put on the "whole Armor of God" and fearlessly enter that battle against the devils schemes. Even in those times when the battle seems hopeless and despair creeps in, the victory ultimately belongs to the Lord Jesus Christ. Be fearless, be strong and be courageous as you enter the battle and wage war against Satan for the heart, mind and soul of your unsaved husband. I believe every wife should add *"Mission Possible"* to her implements of warfare against Satan knowing that if we resist the devil, he will flee.

Maranatha,
Dr. Randy Bryan, President
Binding Broken Hearts Ministries, Inc.
Fleming Island, Florida

You heard from God. Your book is such a blessing to me. I can identify with your words. I can identify with your feelings. I can feel your sincere heart. Throughout the book I found myself saying, "Yes, yes! you are right! I feel that way too!" "I went through that." "I'm dealing with that now!"

This book was truly inspired by God. He chose you to help and encourage other believers in the same situation. Thank you.

Louise Holzendorf Burnam
Author of "Oh No, Not Louise!"

As a Christ-centered Counselor in ministry for over 25 years, I find *Mission Possible* to be an important "must read" book for those who find themselves in a marriage where one partner is saved and the other is not. This would be the beginning of embracing Christ as Husband, and dying to self trying to change the earthly partner. It is in that surrender that one finds true peace and Christ can become Life.

So many marriages go under because no one wants to embrace Galatians 2:20, that the life we now live, we live by THE FAITH OF THE SON OF GOD who LOVED US and GAVE HIMSELF for us. Only when we understand that it is His Faith, not ours, do we begin to appropriate the Word as living reality. Deborah does an excellent job delivering this message. I can only add a word of caution: That is when one is in an abusive relationship where there is physical and mental harm, one is free to depart. Departure is not then necessarily the end, but a time to rest while He works and reveals Truth...Truth that will set you free!

Drucilla Graham, M.A., Pres.
Faith Fellowship Ministries, Inc.
Jacksonville, FL

PREFACE

Your Mission - if you choose to accept it ...

When **GOD** "chooses" you **in the midst of your marriage** as a believer, you have but **one mission to fulfill** - that is believing for your mate's salvation.

Almost every woman in church has a friend who can identify with this book and its message. I am convinced there are many women in our churches who are *waiting* and *believing* for their husband's conversion, yet receive little respect or encouragement for their daunting task of faithfully **"standing in the gap"** for them. This can be one of the hardest areas of church ministry yet one of the most needed. Encouragement to "half of an unsaved couple" is essential.

This book will serve to *encourage your heart*, *strengthen your soul*, and *stretch your faith*.

I believe God's anointing and this book will help to raise a "mighty army of Godly women" who won't give up in the trenches. They will *march into the enemy's camp* shouting! It's time to put the demons in hell on notice that:

"You will be saved, you and your household !" (**Acts 16:31**)

The Author

INTRODUCTION

JESUS - Your Husband's Priestly Model

The writer of the book of Hebrews says, "But Christ [Jesus] came as High Priest of the good things to come, with the greater and more perfect Tabernacle not made with hands, that is, not of this creation" (Heb. 9:11).

JESUS *is* the **perfect role model** for your husband. Some of the duties of a priest in the home are: spiritual covering, leadership (the head), godly authority and correction, repentance on behalf of the family, use of godly wisdom and discernment, servanthood, humility, prayer and intercession, as well as love and care for his family.

The Holy Spirit will "...guide him into all truth" (John 16:13).

Psalm 91 speaks of covering: *"He shall cover you with His feathers, and under His wings you shall take refuge ..."* (vs. 4).

Your husband will be your *"earthly representative"* for your Spiritual Covering. Ephesians 5:23 states, "For the husband is head of the wife, as also Christ is head of the church ..."

As your spiritual covering, your husband has the responsibility to *pray and intercede for you.*

Jesus serves us continually "...ever living to make intercession for us" (Heb. 7:25).

Begin praying now for *"your priest's"* godly qualities of the compassion of Jesus, the goodness of Jesus, the humility of Jesus, the strength of Jesus, and the wisdom of Jesus.

Hebrews 11:1 states: "Now faith is the substance of things hoped for, the evidence of things not seen." Hebrews 11:3 says, "by faith we understand that the worlds were framed by the word of God, so that the things which are seen were not made of things which are visible." By faith, believing for *your husband's* salvation is necessarily a matter of **speaking it into existence**!

> **HOPE** is putting *FAITH*
> "on the line" - and
> *expecting* results!

 *Seek and Find*

1. Jesus is our High Priest and He is your husband's role model. The traditional role of a priest was to offer a blessing (Numbers 6), purify the unclean (Leviticus 15), carry the Ark of the Covenant (Joshua 3), and teach the law (Leviticus 10). Jesus came as the fulfillment of the roles of Prophet, Priest and King. According to the book of Romans, Jesus alone does the following: He satisfies God's justice, pacifies God's wrath, and justifies the sinner. What did Paul have to say in Hebrews 7:22-28? How long will Jesus serve as our priest? For what does Jesus live (see verse 25)? What was sacrificed for us so that we might have eternal representation before God?

2. Jesus came as a man to earth and experienced pain, suffering, and sorrow. He also showed great compassion and empathy for those He served. Read Hebrews 2:17-18. How is Christ able to reach out to your husband and mentor him even if he does not yet know Him intimately? Can you identify qualities in your husband that remind you of Jesus? Do we recognize changes for the better?

3. Without Christ as your Savior, you can possess knowledge and display goodness, but you cannot be "spiritually led". What can wives do in the meantime as we wait for God to work in our husbands? According to Paul, we can pray Ephesians 1:17-19 over our spouse. What does verse 17 say is the key to knowing God? How does that compare to what John says in I John 5:20? Are you convinced that prayer will make a difference in your spouse's life? What did Samuel tell the people in I Samuel 12:23? Do we sin against God when we refuse to pray for our spouse? Why or why not?

How has God spoken to you in your study of the Introduction?

Name some practical steps you can take as you journey with God in your marriage.

Write a prayer to God about *hope*.

Chapter 1

You've Embraced Christ – Now What?

My remarriage in 1982 was *closure* to a lonely period of singleness after being divorced for five years. My new husband was intelligent, caring and romantic, good looking, had a good long-term career, and kept a clean, well organized apartment... That was enough for me!

In the spring of 1989 my neighbor had repeatedly asked me to church and I had repeatedly refused. I didn't need **church** thank you very much, and I politely made numerous excuses. She, however, didn't give up. I eventually gave in and said, "yes", "only for my son's sake," I reminded her. Well, *GOD had other plans !*

I was **radically** saved that first Sunday morning. I had asked many questions in my Sunday school class, and during the invitation, I walked the aisle with my bible study teacher. I remember feeling emotionally worn out that afternoon. I took my son to the park as my husband was working that weekend, and I reflected on all that had transpired. Little did I know God would begin a *work* in **me** that would take me on a spiritual journey I didn't expect.

Day after day, week after week, month after month I grew closer to God, hungered for God and began serving Him from my heart. I took my 2 ½ year old son every time I attended church. My husband would nod his head in approval and wave as we left each week for church.

The **spiritual skirmish** had begun. Don't underestimate the enemy. I did not fully understand spiritual warfare and would learn about that as time progressed. I began to grow in my understanding of God's Word and how Satan opposes a couple's *holy union*. I would learn about **"putting on the whole armor of God"** (Ephesians 6:10-19). I would learn that "**standing firm**" was **mandatory** - - not **an option**. My *spiritual clothing* was necessary for survival as "half of a saved couple". God desires for you to become *"one flesh"* – at the altar and in the spirit realm. Satan can't bear the thought of it. *This* is where your perseverance plays a huge part.

The enemy will mercilessly bombard you with thoughts, feelings, emotions and physical disdain for your mate. You **must** take *every thought captive* (II Corinthians 10:5) and stop looking at your mate as the enemy. Don't let his actions and words provoke you into disobedience.

Paul writes in Ephesians 4:29, "Let no corrupt communication proceed out of your mouth, but what is good for building up, that it may impart grace to the hearers." Matthew 18:9 states, "and if your eye causes you to sin, pluck it out and cast it from you." **So it goes with your tongue.**

Stop committing *spiritual murder* against your mate! Bite it off and cast it away! Don't sin by grieving God as you curse the very person **God wills** to join you to, as **ONE!**

> **ANTICIPATION is our greatest _asset_ in the fulfillment of your spouse's conversion!**

Remember that *"the battle is the **Lord's** " (I Samuel 17:47) and e*arnestly give the salvation of your mate **to God in prayer**. Early on in your conversion it seems easier to be hopeful concerning your husband's salvation. You will need an added **measure of faith** as the years go by.

In Romans 4:18 Paul refers to Abraham by saying, "who, *contrary* to hope, **in hope believed**." This is the type of faith you will need for your husband's salvation.

God is your spiritual husband while your mate is not yet the priest of your home. Your obedience and submission to **Him** are essential as God knows our shortcomings and weaknesses; yet He uses them to perfect us in waiting. Perseverance is one thing you will need with a *"holy dig in your heels"* attitude and a *"stubbornness in the Lord"* towards the salvation of your mate. Salvation is a personal thing. I had responded to The Lord's call, and *my husband had his own choice to make*.

Seek and Find

1. Ephesians 6:10 speaks of being "strong in the Lord and in the power of His might." How does Paul's exhortation compare with what God spoke to Joshua in Joshua 1:9?

2. Ephesians 6:11-12 says to "...put on the whole armor of God, that you may be able to stand against the wiles of the devil." What does verse 12 say about our enemy? Where does the enemy reside? What does Paul say in II Timothy 2:26 about our state of mind and our venerability?

3. In I Samuel 17:37-39 David was blessed and released by King Saul to go fight the giant Goliath. David clothed himself with Saul's armor, helmet, and coat of mail. What happens when we try to go out "to battle" with **natural** armor as opposed to our God-given armor? What made the difference in David's approach to his battle with Goliath (vs. 45-47)? What does Paul say about our armor in II Corinthians 6:7?

4. A good soldier keeps his armor in top condition and checks his weapons frequently for flaws, weaknesses and defects. Ephesians 6:13 says to "take up the whole armor of God..." Read Ephesians 6:14-17 and name each piece of armor and identify its function. Which pieces are defensive in nature, and which ones are offensive? Can we be fully protected if we're missing one piece? Why or why not? According to Hebrews 4:12, what does Paul say about our most important weapon?

5. II Corinthians 10:3-5 teaches that our warfare is spiritual in nature. Natural (or worldly) methods and weapons are not effective. How does this correlate to what Paul addresses in Ephesians 6:12? Remember, your mate is **not** the enemy. How is your obedience to Christ as your "spiritual Commander" effective against the devil's tactics? What is the outcome when we follow God's ways?

6. What is "faith in action"? In James 2:14, James makes the point that we can *say* we have faith. Hebrews 11:1 says, "Now faith is the substance of things hoped for, the evidence of things not seen". How does Hebrews 11:1 compare with Romans 8:24-25? What is James' main point in James 2:17-24? Do you think our part is to help God, or let Him **use us** to bring Him glory?

How has God spoken to you in your study of Chapter 1?

Name some practical steps you can take as you journey with God in your marriage.

Write a prayer to God about *waiting & perseverance*.

Chapter 2

The "Abigail Syndrome"

The traditional story of "Abigail" in I Samuel 25 is a familiar one. Abigail was married to Nabal, a man of means who treated her and everyone else like dirt. Though Nabal was descended from Caleb, he shared none of his virtues. When King David heard that her husband Nabal reviled his men, he was ready to kill him and his household. Abigail went out to meet David with humility and gifts. David highly praised Abigail's courage and advice. Nabal soon died upon hearing what took place after his drunken binge. Abigail became David's wife when he proposed after learning of Nabal's fate. Abigail would now reside with the King in a *"fairy tale"* ending.

Not so fast... Don't be "caught up" in the **Abigail syndrome.** I believe God has a New Testament application for those of us who stand in the gap for our unbelieving husbands. Let's look at what this passage **does not** represent:

We don't pray that our husbands will "drop dead" so we can marry a believer as that would not be in God's perfect will for us. Neither do we hope he'll die from a heart attack to "pay him back" for his evil ways. God has a better plan. I believe this would be the *God honoring* scenario for the wife who believes for her husband's salvation.

> **Divorce *for me* was NOT an
> option. I often said, "I am getting
> a new husband with the
> *same man* - GOD has promised
> me that!**

Abigail was a woman of good understanding. (I Samuel 25:3). Godly wisdom and understanding promote knowing *God's will*. Isaiah 11:2 is a picture of the Holy Spirit for us today:

"The Spirit of the Lord shall rest upon [us], the Spirit of wisdom and understanding, the Spirit of counsel and might, the Spirit of knowledge and the fear of the Lord." We must be in tune with what God would have us do with regards to our mate. Daily prayer and being in God's Word helps us to know God's will.

Interestingly, when David sent his men to ask favor and provision from Nabal, he was indifferent and inquired: "Who is David, and who is the son of Jesse? ... Shall I then take *my bread* and *my water* and *my meat* ... and give it to men when I do not know where they are from?" (I Samuel 25:10-11). Likewise, your husband, just as Nabal, **doesn't know the King yet.**

Often times it is difficult to tithe, attend every church service, or be at every Bible study or function because your husband doesn't *see a need* for you to participate or *share you with God*. Be patient. He must see your **commitment and desire** to be with God's people and in God's presence.

Nabal was a self-made man who was very prideful and greedy. Reading Jesus' parable of the rich fool in Luke 12:16-20, we see similarities.

Nabal was not thankful for anything, nor recognized God's hand of provision at all. Your husband may be **"rich and full of worldly things."** His equating "good things & provision" to GOD are foreign. Only **GOD** can change his heart and priorities as you *pray* for his spiritual enlightenment (Ephesians 1:18). *Pray* for God to woo him by His Spirit into a curiosity and awareness of the things of God.

Unlike King David who planned to wipe out Nabal's lineage, *God has compassion and mercy on our spouses.* He is "not willing that any should perish, but that all should come to repentance" (II Peter 3:9). God *wills* that your spouse join you in **"holy union."** The apostle Paul states in I Corinthians 7:14, 16 "for the unbelieving husband is sanctified by the wife ...for how do you know, O wife, whether you will save your husband?"

When Abigail heard what Nabal had done, she quickly prepared an **offering** for King David. **Our offering brought to our King** is a *humble heart, a willing & submissive spirit, and unwavering obedience.* We **intercede** on our husband's behalf by meeting the **King of Kings.**

> **God *cherishes* the Soul**
> we carry to Him in love
> when it's
> **"one flesh"** we seek.

King David praised Abigail for her *good sense and devotion:* "Blessed be the Lord God of Israel, who sent you this day to meet me! And blessed is your advice and blessed *are you* , because you have kept me this day from coming to bloodshed … unless you had hastened and come to meet me, surely by morning light no males would have been left to Nabal" (I Samuel 25:32-34). David would have wiped out Nabal's name but it was **God's desire to** *"promote a Godly lineage."* Abigail's actions and attitude spared Nabal but Nabal didn't recognize her sacrifice. Our sacrifice on our spouse's behalf is **unwavering faith and persistent prayers** offered up to the Throne of Grace. *GOD always takes notice of devotion!*

Nabal died soon after hearing the whole matter; "His heart died within him, and he became like a stone" (I Samuel 25:37). The world does make man like stone and **cold to the things of God.** *Pray* for your husband as in Ezekiel 36:26: "I will give you a new heart and put a new spirit within you; I will take the heart of stone out of your flesh and give you a heart of flesh." *His spiritual death needs to be recognized by his flesh.* When your husband dies to himself, it will be so **God** can *raise him up with* **"resurrection power"** to be the Godly priest of your home [God] intended! Just as David took Abigail to be his wife, *so your husband* will take unto himself a wife as **God intended** to be, spiritually joined in Holy union. *"…and they shall become one flesh"* (Genesis 2:24).

> *One Heart, One Mind,*
> *One Spirit, One Flesh*

God is faithful. "Lord, help our unbelief !" (Mark 9:24)

Seek and Find

1. Numbers 13 and 14 give us an overview of Moses' command to Joshua and the twelve spies to investigate the land of Canaan, and the subsequent disobedience of the children of Israel in the eyes of the Lord. Caleb has been praised as being virtuous and courageous. Using the passages in Numbers 13:30 and 14:6-9, cite examples that prove that statement. What commendation did the Lord give Caleb in Numbers 14:24?

2. Read I Samuel 25:2-3. How does Nabal's character and pride contrast with that of Caleb? When King David's men approached Nabal to seek favor and provision for their troops, how did he respond in verses 10-12? Is there a similarity between this passage and Jesus' parable in Luke 12:13-21? Abigail "interceded" for Nabal as she went before King David. Verse 25 gives us a clue to Nabal's reputation. What does Proverbs 14:33 and Proverbs 15:2 say about foolish comments and judgments? How can we guard ourselves against foolish actions?

3. Nabal was told about Abigail's intervention the morning after his drunken feast (vs. 36-37) Nabal never showed remorse for his actions. God "struck" Nabal and he died (v. 38). Nabal had no reverence for the things of God or His earthly representative (King David). How does that correlate with what Paul tells the Jews in Romans 2:4-9? We know that God is merciful with those who are indifferent and reject Him. What does II Peter 3:9 say regarding God's promise of redemption? Abigail was generous in her actions by not only covering Nabal's mistakes, but also in her efforts to honor King David and his men. How does Paul exhort us to do the same in Philippians 2:3-4? Grace is a picture of love in action, with no thought of self. How can we serve our husbands and show grace to them when they don't deserve it? How does that bring honor to God in the end?

4. God takes notice of our continual prayers lifted in faith on behalf of our spouse. What does Luke 18:1-8 say about praying in faith? Do you think God gets tired of hearing from us about the same thing over and over? Why or why not? What does Hebrews 11:6 say about God and faith? How does Paul "sum it all up" in I Thessalonians 5:17?

How has God spoken to you in your study of Chapter 2?

Name some practical steps you can take as you journey with God in your marriage.

Write a prayer to God about *spiritual unity*.

Chapter 3

Faith as a Mustard Seed

Jesus said, "To what shall we liken the kingdom of God? Or with what parable shall we picture it? It is like a mustard seed which, when it is sown on the ground, is smaller than all the seeds on the earth; but when it is sown, it grows up and becomes greater than all herbs, and shoots out large branches, so that the birds of the air may nest under its shade" (Mark 4:30-32). When we have faith so small it seems insignificant, God can grow it into something sturdy and supportive that even others can "nest in". In Matthew 17:20 Jesus again says "… for assuredly, I say to you, if you have *faith* as a **mustard seed**, you will say to this mountain, 'Move from here to there,' and it will move; and **nothing** will be impossible for you." All things are possible with God!

One of my daily devotionals, "Streams in the Desert" by L.B. Cowman, has an entry by an unknown author named C.H.P. He talks about a passage written by Paul in the book of Galatians: "Before this faith came, we were held prisoners … locked up until faith should be revealed" (Gal. 3:23 NIV). We are *set aside* for a time to learn a more excellent way of faith.

Moses, Joseph, Paul, Silas, and even John all learned about being *"put aside"* for a season to be locked-up to faith. Commit your circumstances to God. praise Him, and claim Romans 8:28 that "He will work all things to good for those who love Him and are the called according to His pur-

29

pose." Isaiah 64:4 promises that God "acts on behalf of those who wait for Him." Others will receive insight and blessings because you were "locked-up" to learn *the way of faith*.

Hebrews 11 has been called the "Faith Chapter". Paul writes, "By faith we understand that the worlds were framed by the word of God, so that the things which are seen were not made of things which are visible" (Hebrews 11:3). We can *frame* our husband with the Word of God by speaking *into existence* his salvation. God's Word will not return void. Isaiah 46:11 states, "Indeed I have spoken it; I will also bring it to pass. I have purposed it; I will also do it." II Corinthians 1:20 states "For all the promises of God in Him are Yes, and in Him Amen, to the glory of God through us." Amen means *so be it!* God doesn't promise and fall through.

I recommend speaking varied scriptures for salvation over your husband daily. One of my favorite scriptures is Romans 10:20, where Paul quotes a passage from Isaiah 65:1, "I was *found* by those who did not *seek* Me; I was made *manifest* to those who did not *ask* for Me."

This scripture gives me great hope that although my husband isn't looking, God can **find him** and "show Himself" at any time to my husband.

I believe God will *move heaven and earth* to accomplish this task by wooing our husbands "by His Spirit" (Zech 4:6). It is God's job to make that call of salvation and we must pray they hear the "knock." Jesus said, "Behold, I stand at the door and knock. If anyone hears My voice and opens the door, I will come in to him and dine with him, and he with Me" (Rev. 3:20). I pray, "Lord, let him have ears to hear Your knock." In Matthew 19:26, Jesus says, "With men this is impossible but with God *all things are possible*."

Fair weather **Faith** is
Not Faith at all.

Charles H. Spurgeon

The book of the Prophet Ezekiel speaks of the "things that should be hereafter" and has a great similarity to the book of Revelation by the Apostle John. One passage in Chapter 37 depicts the "valley of dry bones" in which God tells the prophet to "prophesy" to the disjointed and dispersed bones. God miraculously brought the "bones to life" joining them with sinews and flesh and skin. Afterwards, God "breathed the breath of life" into them and they became an exceedingly great army!

God can surely breathe the breath of spiritual life *into your husband*! We need to "prophesy" every time we pray that God will raise him up! Speak it into existence! Salvation is a *resurrection to the dead flesh of the world*. Call him forth *by name* and believe that God hears your cry! You need both *prayer* and *the Word* to bring it to pass. It is God's *grace* that will bring it into being. God will not only bring the bones to life, He will "*fashion them into a God ordained man, ready for service*". Ezekiel realized God is the master of the impossible (Ezekiel 37:3). Be ready to accept the improbable, and expect God to "do exceedingly abundantly above all that we ask or think" (Ephesians 3:20).

I am the first to heed the call of salvation in *my* family, but not the last! Psalm 68:6 states "God sets a **solitary one** in a family". I will **stand in the gap** for my unsaved loved ones & claim their lives for Christ! What a privilege it is to carry them to the Throne of Grace and petition God on their behalf! *You'd better take seriously the "holy charge" that has been placed on you.*

You may be the only *"gospel"* they see and hear! The Apostle Peter states in I Peter 3:15, "But sanctify the Lord God in your hearts, and *always be ready* to give a defense to everyone who asks you a reason for the hope that is in you, with meekness and fear ..." Your deep, abiding joy regardless of circumstances is a magnet to those around you who don't yet know the Lord. Remember, we *walk by faith* (II Corinthians 5:7).

> *...not what we see*
> *...not what we hear*
> *...not what we feel*
> *...not what we think*

In Luke 8:48, Jesus says, "Daughter, be of good cheer; your *faith* has made you well [cured]. Go in peace." We need to be *cured of our unbelief.*

It is
GOD's Reputation
"on the line"...
Not yours...
Just believe!

 *Seek and Find*

1. We may often say we have faith, but do we really display it? Read Luke 7:2-10. What did the centurion do in an act of faith to heal his servant? Did he go and meet with Jesus himself? Why or why not? Did that stop Jesus from granting his request on behalf of his servant? How was the centurion's faith demonstrated and what was Jesus' response (v. 9)?

2. When God called Abram to leave Haran and relocate with his family, he did not have a destination revealed to him. Paul says in Hebrews 11:8, "By faith Abraham obeyed when he was called to go out to the place where he would *afterward* receive as an inheritance. And he went out, not knowing where he was going". Oswald Chambers, in his devotional, *My Utmost for His Highest* says, "Faith never knows where it is being led, but it loves and knows the One Who is leading." God may be leading you to an unknown place in your marriage and in your walk with Him. What does I John 4:18 say about love and fear? How do we know we can trust what God says? What does Hebrews 10:23 say with regards to God's character?

3. Jesus said, "Behold, I stand at the door and knock. If anyone hears My voice and opens the door, I will come in to him and dine with him, and he with Me" (Revelation 3:20). We know that God's Spirit woos us to Himself and that we are "sought after" by God. What is said about our worth to God in Luke 19:10 and Matthew 18:11-13? Compare I Timothy 2:4 and II Peter 3:9 to find out who God promises to save and if anyone is excluded. What does Jesus say in Luke 15:10 about those who know Him as Savior?

4. Psalm 68:6 says, "God sets a solitary one in families". Believers are to stand in the gap for our unsaved loved ones. Paul and Luke held a Sabbath prayer meeting in Philippi on the banks of a river (Acts 16:14-15) Name the woman who heard the Word of truth. Do you think she had any influence over others in her household? Why or why not? What about the ruler of the synagogue in Acts 18:7-8? Justus lived next door to the synagogue. Do you think he had any influence over Crispus and his decision to follow God? We too can influence others!

How has God spoken to you in your study of Chapter 3?

Name some practical steps you can take as you journey with God in your marriage.

Write a prayer to God about *faith*.

Chapter 4

Painful Reality

"But as for me and my house, we will serve the Lord" (Joshua 24:15). How confident I was that soon "all would be well with my house." Little did I know that years would go by with little change. My husband was a good moral man: he loved his family and was deeply devoted; he loved and cared for his parents; he loved and respected his in-laws; he was a hard worker, responsible, didn't drink, smoke or chase women. "What a great Christian he'll make," I thought. Sadly, he wasn't interested in the "things of God." He didn't care to socialize with the "church crowd." He attended church services occasionally, but never talked about God. What was I to do?

Whatever you do, don't be a modern day *Jonah* and try to run away from your **God appointed mission**. There will be direct conflict with "your will" over what to do. The Prophet Jonah didn't want to go to Nineveh for many reasons, but none of them were good enough for God. (*Your reason won't be either*).

You must have a genuine love for his soul because he is your husband and that is who will spend eternity with you. When Jonah had pity on the plant more than the inhabitants of Nineveh, God rebuked him saying, "You have had pity on the plant for which you have not labored, nor made it grow ... and should I not pity Nineveh, that great city, in which are more than one hundred and twenty thousand persons who cannot discern between their right hand and their left?" (Jonah 4:10-11). Likewise, with regards to your husband, have pity *on his soul*. Jesus died as much for *him* as for you. Pray that God will enlarge your gift of compassion towards him. Pray for a "burden for his soul". Pray for God's mercy. Someone cared about *your* soul enough to point you to Christ.

> My husband had a
> **"target on his back"**
> and wasn't aware that **GOD**
> *had His arrow of LOVE*
> **"aimed right at the bulls eye"!**

John 15:5 says, "I am the vine, you are the branches. He [she] who abides in Me, and I in [her] bears much fruit; for without Me you can do nothing." God's spirit *draws* your mate to Himself. Your spiritual *fruit* is what is visible when you are abiding in and drawing life from God.

Your husband will unknowingly be drawn "to the things of God *in you*" completely unaware of God's sovereignty in all circumstances. Your fruit of the spirit: *love, joy, peace, longsuffering, kindness, goodness, faithfulness, gentleness, and self-control* (Galatians 5:22-23) all serve to point your husband (unaware) to God. He will notice the difference, but not be able to pin-point when it happened or why. He might never verbalize the change he sees, but he will notice. Let's not fool ourselves, we know we don't live 24 hrs. a day with spiritual fruit hanging all over us – *come on.* Nonetheless, let us strive to display fruit here and there to pique the lost to curiosity! Proverbs 31:25-27 says,

"Strength and honor are her clothing; *she shall rejoice in time to come*. She opens her mouth with wisdom, and on her tongue is the law of kindness. She watches over the ways of her household, and does not eat the bread of idleness." Let us *strive* to be godly women of worth.

Another eye-opener is how your obedience to God and His principles are the *key* to opening the "gate" for your mate into the kingdom of heaven. "Behold, to *obey* is better than sacrifice ..." (I Samuel 15:22). God is **not** moved by your circumstances, crying, discomfort, whining, pity parties, anger or disappointment . He is, however, moved with compassion by your *faith,* your *faithfulness*, and your *devotion* to Him. Your obedient prayers of faith and prayers of intercession for his soul please God. Your husband *lingers in the valley of decision* (Joel 3:14) so his decision will be based, in part, on a perception of God and His place in *your* life. A Godly example *is* the best teacher. Keep praying for God to reveal Himself more and more to your husband in every area of life, work, leisure, provision, and activity.

Sometimes even Christians can be cruel. There are some who would take the verse: "Do not be unequally yoked together with unbelievers." as *proof* not to stay married. "For what fellowship has righteousness with lawlessness? And what communion has light with darkness?" (II Corinthians 6:14). Paul was not discussing marriage. I believe Paul was addressing problems in the church at Corinth caused by mixing believers and unbelievers in business, in worship, in fellowship, and day to day decisions. Believers should not willingly "join themselves to unbelievers" in marriage as that leads to *spiritual disunity*.

When one spouse in the marriage **finds the Lord first**, that is addressed by Paul in I Corinthians 7:10-16, "Now to the married I command, *yet* not I but the Lord: A wife is not to depart from *her* husband. But even if she does depart, let her remain unmarried or be reconciled to *her* husband... But to the rest, I, not the Lord, say: And a woman who has a husband who does not believe, if *he is willing to live with her,* let her not divorce him. For the unbelieving husband is sanctified by the wife , ... otherwise your children would be unclean, but now they are holy. But if the unbeliever departs, let him depart; a brother or sister is not under bondage in such cases. But God has called us to peace. *For how do you know, O wife, whether you will save your husband? ...*" Quite a lot to contemplate, don't you think ?

There will be unsaved family and friends that will think you're crazy for staying with him. They say it's a waste of time – get a divorce and be happy. Problem is, you're a *child of God* and *we don't do things the world's way*! "... that **our faith** should **not** be in the *wisdom of men,* but in the *power of God*" (I Corinthians 2:5).

Oswald Chambers, in his daily devotional *"My Utmost For His Highest"* writes about faith contradicting common sense:

> "On the mount it is easy to say – 'Oh, yes, I believe God can do it'; but you have to come down into the demon-possessed valley and meet with facts that laugh ironically at the whole of your mount-of-transfiguration belief. Every time my programme of belief is clear to my own mind, I come across something that contradicts it. Let me say I believe God will supply all my need, and

then let me run dry, with no outlook, and see whether I will go through the trial of faith, or whether I will sink back to something lower. Faith must be tested, because it can be turned into a personal possession only through conflict. What is your faith up against just now? The test will either prove that your faith is right, or it will kill it... The final thing is confidence in Jesus. Believe steadfastly on Him and all you come up against will develop your faith."

Many times, in discouragement I would say, "God, I can't do this anymore; I'm too tired." Then I would hear God speak to my heart, " Yes, I know you are ... just rest in Me and leave this at My altar. My grace is sufficient for you... My strength is made perfect *in your weakness*" (II Corinthians 12:9). He would say "Come to Me, *all* you who labor and are heavy laden [weary], and I will give you rest" (Matthew 11:28). Verse 29 specifically says "rest for your *souls.*" Jesus says, "Take My yoke upon you and learn from Me, for I am gentle and lowly in heart, and you will find rest for your souls." Our soul is our mind, our will and our emotions. How we desperately need rest for those! The battle in those areas weaken us and takes its toll mentally & physically. "The **spirit** indeed *is* willing, but the **flesh** *is* weak" (Matthew 26:41). We just need to *keep on keeping o*n with **patient perseverance**.

> This is a *day to day battle*. If I didn't **believe** that a Holy Ghost supply-line was on its way, *I couldn't last another day!*

Another area of battle is coping with the daily changes that occur within yourself, and how that interacts with your mate. As a *"child of light"*, you begin to see life differently *through God's filter*. Things of the world no longer satisfy, excite, or challenge you. Your sights are set *higher*. Part of that is reflected in your relationship – as a wife, friend and lover. There unfortunately are things that you begin to dislike about him. We are to "love the sinner, but hate the sin." There were times I had to pray, "Lord, give me a *desire* for my husband … help me to love him with *Your love,* because I don't like him very much right now." Remember, you have to "take every thought captive, unto the obedience of Christ" (II Corinthians 10:5). Give it to God and then you will have peace. Isaiah 3:26 says, "You will keep him [her] *in perfect peace,* whose mind is stayed on You, because he trusts in You." "Let not your heart be troubled …" (John 14:1). You will have peace when you give these struggles to God, and *let Him keep them*.

> **Great faith
> has peace
> for it's friend.**

Radical faith requires radical steps! Many times I would do things while in a "warring prayer mode" that to the normal person would seem strange. Satan would love for us to stay passive and non-threatening, but you'd better trash any ideas about "playing fair" with the enemy! He sure doesn't play fair with us!

Whenever my husband would be at work, (or while away on business) I would "charge my home atmosphere" by playing *praise & worship* music and begin to pray and *"prophesy into existence"* how he would be. This takes real faith and Holy Spirit leading. I would pray and then verbalize scripturally how he would be *"as a new creature in Christ"* knowing that God's Word does not return void or empty. I would lay his Bible (which I never saw him read) in his easy chair, opened to the scripture I was claiming for him (Romans 10:20). Paul quotes Isaiah: "I was found by those who did not seek Me; I was made manifest to those who did not ask for Me."

This is an example of my conversation:

"I thank you, Lord, that my husband will be a mighty man of God; a man so in love with you that he will not be able to satisfy the hunger he has for you... he will reach for his Bible instead of the *TV remote*, he will desire to be with your people and enjoy their fellowship. He will be the priest of his home and take on his priestly duties with godly reverence. He will pray with his family and long to serve you the rest of his days. Thank you, Lord, that he will desire to *"dwell in Your presence"* and enjoy the things of God. Thank you, Lord that you will take the craving for the world away from him and replace it with an appetite for You. Thank you, Lord that you are bringing it to pass. In Jesus name it is done!"

That's the kind of faith God wants us to have! When we continue to believe for it, even though we don't see it (Hebrews 11:1)! Hebrews 10:23 states, "Let us hold fast the confession of our *hope without wavering*, for He who *promised* is *faithful*."

It's a matter of ***trusting God***. "Trust in the Lord with all your heart, and lean *not* on your own understanding" (Proverbs 3:5). Trusting God with your husband ***is an act of spiritual worship***.

 *Seek and Find*

1. Read Jonah 1:1-2. God gave Jonah a mission. Jonah was a prophet from the northern kingdom of Israel. He was a contemporary of Jeroboam II and ministered after the time of Elisha. Nineveh was a wicked place and Jonah was not going to preach there if he could avoid it. But that was not his decision. God intervened and Jonah relented (Jonah 1:4 – 2:10). After Jonah obeyed God and saw the fruit of his labor (Jonah 3), God used a plant, a worm, and the wind to teach Jonah a lesson in compassion (Jonah 4). What does God have to use to get our attention when it comes to our spouse? Do you "run the other way" when God asks you to veer into uncertain territory?

2. Contrast Jonah with the apostle Paul. In Act 16:6-7 Paul and Silas tried to preach in a particular area of Asia. God had shut the door, but opened another in Macedonia. How did Paul and Silas respond to God's prompting in verses 9-10? What do you think would have been the outcome if Jonah had heeded his call and obeyed God the first time? What do we learn about God and His sovereignty? Do you think God can do whatever it takes to reach your spouse for Him? Why or why not?

3. II Corinthians 12:9 says, "...My strength is made perfect in weakness." Jesus told us in Matthew 11:29 to "Take My yoke upon you and learn from Me, for I am gentle and lowly in heart, and you will find rest for your souls." What promise does He give us in verse 30? What does David say in Psalm 23:2-3 that leads you to believe that Jesus requires us to rest and be refreshed in order to be useful in His kingdom?

4. When we are tempted to rise up in our flesh and react to a difficult situation without first seeking God's direction, what is the likely outcome? What does Philippians 4:6-7 say about the relationship between prayer and peace? What does peace guard according to verse 7? Where do our emotions and reactions emerge from? What does Peter say in I Peter 3:11? How are we to pursue peace in our households, without causing spiritual upheaval at its expense? Jesus told us in Matthew 5:9 that we are blessed if we are peacemakers. How does Paul address living the peaceful life in Romans 12:18? What is our responsibility? What other Godly characteristic does Paul say we need to have in Hebrews 12:14 in order to pursue peace?

5. When Jesus said we are to "abide in Him... and bear much fruit..." we think of Paul's writing in the fifth chapter of Galatians. Fruit is either green and immature, or it is ripe and appealing. You spouse looks at your orchard every day. What will he see? In Matthew 5:13-16, Jesus likens believers' lives to a city on a hill, which cannot be hidden. What happens when you look out in the distance, to a city in the dark of night? If we are called to be children of light and reflect Christ's glory to others, how can we keep that flame "glowing?"

How has God spoken to you through Chapter 4?

What practical steps can you take as you journey with God in your marriage?

Write a prayer to God about *trust* and *faithfulness*.

Chapter 5

Timing is Everything !

"To everything *there is* a season, a time for every purpose under heaven ..." (Ecclesiastes 3:1). God is never early and never late, but always on time. Your husband's salvation securely lies within His loving arms and rests on His promises.

In Chapter 16 of I Samuel, David was anointed in the midst of his brothers as the new King of Israel. Years passed before it became reality. Time is of no concern to God, unless it is in His will to *direct* it. God orchestrates circumstances to accomplish all that He determines to do. David had to go through many **hardships and heartaches** *before* God allowed him to rightfully take his throne. He was anointed king in Hebron, first over the house of Judah, then over the house of Israel, uniting the two kingdoms. II Samuel 5:1 states that when the ten tribes said they would "reunite" with the two tribes, they said, "Indeed we *are* your bone and your flesh." What a beautiful picture of the spiritual *rejoining* of both parts of a covenant. God had said to David, "You shall shepherd My people Israel, and be ruler over Israel." When God's perfect timing occurs, *you* will be reunited in the Spirit and the covenant of *spiritual oneness* will be sealed. You will be *one flesh* and *one spirit.* You will then be "equally yoked", as God intended. You cannot hurry God's divine plan nor appointment for your husband. It must be left in His hands, for God draws him by His Spirit (Zech. 4:6).

King David's own Psalm 30 speaks of a dramatic deliverance. Verses 4-5 are a picture of God's grace in a time of waiting, "Sing praise to the Lord, you saints of His, and give thanks at the remembrance of His holy name. For His anger is but for a moment, His favor is for life; Weeping may endure for a night, *But joy comes in the morning*." How beautiful will be the morning **when your husband surrenders to God** !

> # GOD is relentless
> ### in a *loving pursuit*
> ### of your **mate!**

Another wonderful example of God's perfect timing is in the book of Esther. When Queen Vashti refused to come before King Ahasuerus when summoned, I believe God allowed her disobedience and *attitude* to be used for His glory. She set in motion a decree that would dethrone her and send the King's court "looking for a new replacement."

Esther had been carried away with her cousin, Mordecai, during the days of captivity in Persia. God had her *in the right place*, *at the right time*. When the King and his assistant gathered all the "eligible young women" for his choosing, Esther was among them. After six months of preparation with oil of myrrh, and six months with perfumes and beauty treatments, each one was presented to the King. Esther was favored over all the other virgins presented to the King, and he set the royal crown upon *her* head and made her queen.

Likewise, God is *"working behind the scenes"* with your husband. The time spent waiting is both for *his* benefit <u>and</u> for *yours*. Just as Esther spent much time in preparation for an audience with the King, so too are you being readied. God does a **"refining work"** in *you*, as He brings your *spouse* **closer to the King**. God is preparing *the bride of Christ in you* for the day He joins you two as one in the spiritual realm. Your husband is being **groomed** for his *true* wedding vows. **God** will officiate over the sacred event and pronounce a *blessing over you*.

When Esther learned that plans had been approved by the King to destroy the Jews throughout the land, she was instructed by Mordecai to approach the King and plead their case. She knew that if the King did not extend his scepter to her, she would be killed. No one would escape the wrath of the King, **including Esther**. Mordecai warned her, "For if you remain completely silent at this time, relief and deliverance will arise for the Jews from another place, but you and your father's house will perish. *Yet who knows whether you have come to the kingdom for such a time as this?" (Esther 4:14).*

You too have a choice to make – will you ignore the fact that your husband's salvation is a matter for **you** to become involved (*i.e. prayer, fasting, witnessing), or do you ignore it and let God use someone else to reach him? I don't know about you*, but **I** want to know that, when the time comes, I will be ready and **stand in the gap**! I don't want to grieve God by turning my head and let the chips *fall where they may.*

So Esther and her maids fasted and prayed before she entered the King's presence. Esther knew this was serious business. It was against the law to do what she was willing to do ... even onto death! That is what she was willing to do - *die*. We have to be ready to **"die"** to ourselves, our timetable, and our idea of *when God, when?* Put it all on the altar and **leave it there**! I am reminded of a toddler who has in his possession a pair of scissors... to him they are a toy. But mom says, "give me the scissors." The child screams, crying, shaking his head, clenching his fist, stomping his feet, saying, **"NNOOOOooO !! It's MINE !!"** If we don't have the *faith* to **let go** and give it to God. God **can't** move on our behalf. We must be willing to trust God. Esther was *willing* to trust and God delivered!

Keep the Outcome in mind.
What will bring God
the most Glory?

Another example of God's perfect timing is in the 11th chapter of John. Lazarus was well known in the town of Bethany. His sisters, Martha and Mary, extended hospitality to Jesus during his visits there. He had a close bond with them.

Lazarus was very ill and therefore, Martha and Mary sent word to Jesus of his condition. Jesus loved Martha and Mary very much. He knew God's timetable would be misunderstood but He told those with the news, "This sickness is not unto death, but for the glory of God, that the *Son of God may be glorified through it*" (John 11:4). Jesus actually stayed in Bethabara beyond the Jordan for **2 more days** before coming to Bethany. Jesus told his disciples that

"Lazarus sleeps, but I go that I may wake him up" (John 11:11). (They thought he was sleeping due to sickness and would awake) But Jesus plainly said to them, "**Lazarus is dead**. And I am glad for your sakes that I was not there, *that you may believe*. Nevertheless let us go to him" (vs. 14-15).

God sometimes has to speak plainly to us... **Your husband is spiritually dead** – not just sleeping. We need to look hard into the face of reality. *Either there is fruit or there is not* (Matthew 7:16, 20). Jesus also said that because they would be with Him upon His return to Lazarus, they would believe then! Jesus will bring us with Him that we might also *see and believe...*

When your husband is
so dead you know there's
no hope, that is when
GOD will do a
Miracle!

Following Lazarus' death, Mary & Martha had many comforting friends visit with them, and Jews from Jerusalem also came to pay their respects to the family. However, when Martha heard that Jesus was enroute to their home, she went to meet Him on the road. Mary stayed in the house, sitting in grief and disbelief. Martha quickly told Jesus, "Lord, if You had been here, my brother would not have died" (verse 21). The next few verses give a dialog between Martha and Jesus that is interesting. Martha says, "But even **now** I know that whatever You ask of God, *God* *will give You*." Martha still had great faith in who Jesus was and the power He held. Martha and Jesus discussed the **resurrection to come** and Martha declared her belief that He was indeed the Messiah. Little did she understand that **Jesus** *is* the *Resurrection and the Life* – **Now and Forever**!

Martha told Mary that Jesus had come to see her, and Mary ran to meet Him on the road outside of Bethany. The Jews thought she was running to the grave site to continue her mourning. Mary met Jesus and seeing Him, fell at His feet, and said to Him, "Lord, if You had been here, my brother would not have died" (John 11:21).

In the natural realm, **Jesus is with your spouse** – He just isn't *recognized by him yet*. Your spouse died in sin and now Jesus wants to *resurrect him*. I Corinthians 2:14 says, "But the natural man does not receive the things of the Spirit of God, for they are foolishness to him; nor can he know *them*, because they are spiritually discerned." **Death** can be the gateway to **life** for your husband.

When Jesus saw Mary and the other Jews weeping, He groaned in the spirit and became troubled (John 11:33). When He asked where Lazarus had been laid, they told Him. John 11:35 says, "*Jesus wept*." Then the Jews said, "**See how He loved him !**" (verse 36). **Jesus wept** *for my husband and your husband*. He *is* grieved in His spirit for them. **Are you? Jesus loves souls.**

When Jesus came to the tomb, it was a cave with a stone at the entrance. Verse 39 tells us that Jesus commanded the stone be taken away. Martha was incredulous at the thought.

"Lord, by this time there is a stench, for he has been dead *four* days" (v. 39). Jesus lifted up His eyes to heaven and prayed, asking God's favor on the miracle for "their sakes". He cried out with a loud voice, "**Lazarus, come forth** !" (verse 43). Then he who had **died** came out bound hand and foot with the grave clothes, and Jesus said to them, "Loose him , and let him go" (v.44).

Your spouse is **deader than dead!** He *stinks!* When God calls your husband to Him, it will be with the same **authority,** and **love,** and *perfect timing* as Jesus did with Lazarus! I often "cried out in a loud voice" my husband's name while in intercessory prayer for him. Call him **out of the grave**! Satan wants to keep him there - it's time to fight for his freedom!

> Your husband may be
> **"on lease"** to Satan,
> but he is *God's property* when
> it comes to the "Title"!

God will free your husband from the "**things of the world that bind him up**" and he will *come forth* to be the godly husband he was destined to be! God specializes in *resurrections*! **Nothing** is too difficult for Him (Luke 1:37).

There are times when you might question God's timing. Don't beat yourself up by asking why your prayers haven't been answered yet. Don't let the terrible trio of **fear**, **doubt**,

and unbelief do a number on you. The enemy loves to torture you with those, so don't be double minded (James 1:8). Take authority and **just believe**. Try not to analyze why your spouse won't "take hold of the cross." Was it pride? Anger? Resentment at God?

We are not the Holy Spirit. Only God searches the heart and tests the mind (Jeremiah 17:10). God knows the *perfect timing* and *perfect plans* He has for your husband. "For I know the thoughts that I think towards you, says the Lord, thoughts of peace and not of evil, to give you future and a hope" (Jeremiah 29:11). **Give it over to God *today!***

 *Seek and Find*

1. Read Ruth 1:2-5. Becoming a widow in biblical times meant hardship for most women. Naomi decided to return to Bethlehem with Ruth, her daughter-in-law. What was the season of the year that the two women returned to Naomi's hometown? (v. 22). Read Ruth 2:1-9. The last sentence in verse 3 says, "And she happened to come to the part of the field belonging to Boaz, who was of the family of Elimelech." Do you believe in coincidences, or do you think God possibly orchestrated this "chance" meeting? Read Ruth 2:8-9 and 14-16. How is Boaz's compassion and interest in Ruth portrayed? What was Ruth's response in verse 10? How did Boaz compliment Ruth in vs. 11-12? Boaz became Ruth's kinsman redeemer and married her (Ruth 4:13). We know that Ruth was King David's great-grandmother. Read Matthew 1:5. Who is mentioned in Jesus' genealogy? What does that tell you about God's perfect timing?

2. Read Luke 19:1-10. Jesus knew He would be visiting Jericho on His way to Jerusalem that particular day. Verse 5 tells us that Jesus came to the very place where Zacchaeus was, and looked up. He then said, "Zacchaeus, make haste and come down, for today I must stay at your house" (v. 5). What does that tell you about God's timing? Did Jesus know that Zacchaeus would be waiting in that sycamore tree for Him to pass by? How are your plans and destiny out of your control and safely in the Hands of God? Zacchaeus' name means "*righteous one*". We know he was a chief tax collector and very wealthy. What does Luke 19:8-10 tell us about Zacchaeus' heart and newly found salvation? What happens when we meet Jesus "face to face" unexpectedly? Jesus called him by name and told him He must stay with him (v. 5). How do we respond when God calls out to us, and invites us to "abide" with Him? Are we quick to answer (v. 6), or do we drag our feet and make excuses?

3. Read Matthew 25:1-13. Jesus told this parable to teach his disciples to be prepared and committed to the things of God. What does verse 10 say about timing? Preparation is important for every kingdom purpose. What could the five foolish virgins have done to prepare themselves for the bridegroom in advance (v. 9)? Would there have been a different outcome if they had made better use of their time while the bridegroom was delayed instead of sleeping? Read Mark 13:35 and Matthew 24:36. What does that tell us about our being ready and God's timing? Does God give us instructions on how to prevent "missing the mark" or sinning? What does Ephesians 5:15-17 say about staying in God's will?

4. James 1:6-8 says we are to ask in faith, without doubting, and to not be "double-minded". Why is it important not to waiver, but to be sure and steadfast? How can we stay faithful while waiting on God? What does Daniel 6:26 say about God's kingdom? How should we act in faith according to Colossians 1:23? What does Isaiah 33:6 say about our stability? How does God's Word provide the groundwork for our foundation? Read Matthew 7:24 to find out how we are to build and why.

How has God spoken to you in your study of Chapter 5?

Name some practical steps you can take as you journey with God in your marriage.

Write a prayer to God about *God's perfect timing.*

Chapter 6

In the Meantime - Serve

"… through love serve one another" (Galatians 5:13). "And let us not grow weary while doing good, for in due season we shall **reap,** if we do not lose heart" (Galatians 6:9).

During your time of *"waiting on the Lord"* (Psalm 27:14), you must be courageous. This is not a time for whimpering and whining. This is a time to dig in and <u>serve</u> – and a time to dig trenches and fortify your position in Christ regarding your mate. The enemy is stealthy and clever in distraction regarding your mission. He will try to divert your energy and resources into other areas that might be good, but not **GOD's best!** Be careful with too many church activities and over commitment. Remember, your spouse does not understand your *need* to serve the kingdom purposes. They just don't understand it. Balance is crucial when it comes to home, church, and work. Pray that God will prepare your husband's heart and give you that understanding and favor regarding your "God assignments". Use *spiritual sensitivity and discernment* when it comes to volunteering yourself for everything that comes your way at church. God will affirm to you the right things to do, and conversely, He will squelch those things which are wrong for you at the time. You must stay in touch with God on a daily basis through prayer, reading the Word, and seeking the Spirit's leading to know His will for you and your household. There were many times I would talk to my husband, asking him if he would mind if I attended a conference, took a class, or volunteered for a project. I believe my respect for my husband went a long way. He knew if he really didn't want me to do something (within reason), that I would decline. However, if God made it clear to me that I *must* do something for Him, I would risk the flow of harmony in the home and pursue it with gentle *love and understanding*.

For many years, I faithfully attended church services and served in several areas of ministry: Sunday School, Vacation Bible School, outreach & visitation, Finance Committee, various Bible studies, etc. Spiritual growth and personal commitment to my local church were extremely important to me, as well as being a godly role model for my son. There were many activities I did when my husband was at work, so as not to interfere with "family time" or day to day family obligations.

Every spouse is going to handle your commitment to God differently. Some will get angry, some resentful, some indifferent, some jealous, some relieved (especially workaholics), and the list goes on. Only you know your mate, and only God can work in his heart. "Be wise as a serpent, and gentle as a dove" (Matthew 10:16).

> Your husband is **watching** your
> *level of commitment…*
> **Is it real? Will it last?**
> **Can he see how much you**
> **love *JESUS* and the things of GOD?**

I believe God gives **favor** to the unbelieving husband *on behalf of* the believing wife. God's laws of sowing and reaping are evident when even *one of you* embraces them. I was blessed to be self-employed for a number of years and was able to **tithe** on my income. Since the first year I gave my life to Jesus, I began to tithe to my church regularly. I did not grow up in the church and the concept of tithing was foreign to me. When I heard preaching and teaching on tithing, I knew I had to do it. Knowing that God doesn't need our money, but rather, we give from an over-flowing heart, made it easy for me to give. The idea of sowing into the kingdom of God, and reaping in the heavenly realm made me anxious to see what God would do. Obedience in giving paves the way for God to do marvelous things on your behalf!

Part of my giving has been to those who are involved in the "harvest of souls". I give to individuals and groups who embrace souls and their destiny. I have cheerfully given to Christian radio, Christian TV, many evangelists (local, national & world-wide), and various world outreach mission projects. I have always believed that *sowing for souls is planting seed for my husband.* I have a friend who goes on mission trips, and it is my great pleasure to give her money for the trips. I tell her, "This gift to you is my "*seed*" for my husband's soul, so go preach the good news for a harvest of souls !"

Another area of sowing & reaping is *in prayer*. When you begin to **pray for another woman's husband**, you are **sowing seed for your harvest**. Pray in faith, believing for her miracle! Pray, calling her husband by name into the kingdom and pray for his spiritual enlightenment. Pray that God will raise him up to be the godly husband he should be.

Pray with fervency, conviction, and with certainty that God will answer and it will come to pass. Pray believing for him as you would for your spouse! *Sow seed for your miracle!*

I foresee women in churches around the country form-ing *MISSION POSSIBLE Prayer Groups* and standing in agreement for their husbands! God embraces our unity in the spirit, and being unified, woman to woman for each hus-band's salvation - that is **powerful!** God expects us to **storm heaven on their behalf**! So, watch out Satan, because we're not going to sit back and let you wreak havoc on our homes anymore. **We're claiming** our **households for Christ!** Our husbands *will serve the Lord! Amen!* Matthew 11:12 states, "And from the days of John the Baptist until now The Kingdom of heaven suffers violence, **and the violent take it by force.**"

Satan sees your mission as
a *"joke"*,
but GOD sees it
as **"Mission Accomplished"**!

Beware, that while you are busy serving and waiting, often the enemy will delight in torturing you with thoughts of defeat. You'll be sitting in church, watching the other couples and think, "Lord, what about them?" "They've got each other, Lord..." "When is it going to be my turn?"

And the Lord would answer **me**, "What is that to you? **You follow me.**" The Apostle Peter questioned the Lord about John and Jesus told him, "If I will that he remain till I come, what is that to you? *You* follow me" (John 21:21-22). We need to have an *attitude of gratitude* and not question God's authority and sovereignty. We *are* human and we will have days when we're discouraged and down, but we must encourage ourselves in the Lord as David did in Psalm 42:11, "Why are you cast down, O my soul? And why are you disquieted within me? Hope in God; For I shall yet praise Him, The help of my countenance and my God." If we never had anything else to praise God for *except our salvation*, we should be a most **grateful people**!

I Peter 5:7 says, [in humility] "casting all your care upon Him, for He cares for you." Sometimes we have *many concerns and burdens* to cast upon Him. There are days we must ask God to forgive us for an attitude that is less than honorable. When my husband hurt me with a comment or action, I would find myself saying to God, "Forgive him, Lord, for he knows not what he does." We cannot afford to hold a grudge and give place to the devil. We must be peacemakers. Matthew 5:9 says, "Blessed are the peacemakers, for they shall be called sons of God." Love is the "bond of perfection" and you must "let the peace of God rule in your hearts ..." (Colossians 3:14-15). We need to remind ourselves that "we wrestle not against flesh and blood, but against principalities, against powers, against the rulers of the darkness of this age, against spiritual hosts of wickedness in the heavenly places" (Ephesians 6:12). Your husband is **not** the enemy – *Satan is!*

I often longed to share the intimate things of God with him, but could not. "But the **natural man** does not receive the things of the Spirit of God, for they are foolishness to him; nor can he know them, because they are spiritually discerned" (I Corinthians 2:14); and "... what communion has light with darkness?" (II Corinthians 6:14). So I would *prophetically* say, "Thank you, Lord, that my husband will be a mighty man of God, cherishing the things of God. I thank you that he will be "on fire" – desiring to serve you and recognize your perfect plan for his life. Make me the Godly wife I need to be – a helpmeet to him that pleases you, Lord."

When a single friend of mine said to pray for her, so that "she could wait on God for the right man - - the best man; a mighty man of prayer and a heart for God," I was thinking to myself, "Amen, sister ... **now pray that for me!**" **Can I wait**? Surely God will do a supernatural work in *my* husband! Time means nothing when God does the training-up. When my husband spoke of his retirement, I *claimed by faith* that He would **be freed up to serve God with me**, and he would bask in God's presence in all that *free time*. **Now that's believing for God to move**!

Whenever I caught myself in a "pity party," I would read Psalm 119:28: "My soul melts from heaviness; strengthen me according to Your word." "Great is *Your* faithfulness; The Lord is my portion ... therefore *I hope in Him*" (Lamentations 3:23-24). As the Apostle Paul said in Philippians 3:13-14, "...but one thing I do, forgetting those things which are behind and reaching forward to those things which are ahead, I press toward the goal for the prize of the upward call of God in Christ Jesus."

Focus on God and your eye on the prize - *GOD does!*

 *Seek and Find*

1. Galatians 5:13 says we are to "through love serve one another." There will be times when you don't *feel* like serving your spouse, much less talk to him. Remember, your spouse sees you as a representative of Jesus. You are an ambassador of Christ. What advice does Paul give in Ephesians 4:29-32? Is that a hard thing to do given the nature of your relationship, when only one of you is a believer? What does Philippians 4:8 say about our thought life? How can that impact our words and actions? Read verse 13. Where does our strength come from in order to be more like Jesus?

2. When things at home become "heated", how do you respond to your spouse? How does Paul encourage us to act in Galatians 5:16-17? James says the tongue is a small part of the body, but it can do great damage. How does he characterize it in James 3:8-10? What does Proverbs 21:23 say about our words? Read Proverbs 31:26. What is the key to saying "all the right things?" What does James say about Godly wisdom in James 3:17? How do we obtain that wisdom and claim it as our own?

3. While we are waiting for our miracle, God is using the time to mature us in the things of the Lord. One thing God teaches us is patience as He works out His will in our marriage. James 5:7-8 explains to us that patience is seen in nature as the farmer waits for the seed to grow into mature fruit. Seedtime and harvest are principles that God has set forth in His kingdom and on earth. Patience has rewards. Read James 1:4. What does James say we gain in waiting on God? Does maturity come quickly, or does it take experience and time? How do waiting and trust work together? In Genesis 15:4 God promised Abram an heir from his own body. Abram waited many years for that promise. Read Genesis 16:1-2. How did Sarah *help* God's plan along? Do you think Abram trusted God and His plan? Why or why not? Do you think it was an easy thing for Abram to wait patiently for the promise? What does Psalm 27:13 say about waiting.

4. God will often use something extraordinary to "test us" and refine us in His furnace of love. Evangelist Stephen Hill wrote in his devotional, *Daily Awakenings,* "Do not resent these times of refining. The heat may be intense, but the results will be immense." Obtaining pure gold or silver is painstakingly slow. Taking a shortcut could result in an inferior metal. What does Malachi 3:3 say about what we can offer the Lord during our process of purification and refinement? When God removes the "dross" of our life, what remains? What did Job have to say about God's testing in Job 23:10? Our testimony before God is precious as gold. Gold has historically been a symbol of purity and majesty. In Exodus 37 we have the pattern set forth by God for the items that were in the Holy of Holies: the Ark of the Covenant, the Table of Showbread, the Gold Lampstand and the Altar of Incense. Pure gold was used for all of them. In Revelation chapter 21, verse 15 says the angel had a "gold reed" that he used to measure the city, its gates and its wall. What does verse 18 say the city was made of? What does Psalm 19:10 say about God's words and works? How does the author of Psalm 119:72 describe it?

How has God spoken to you through Chapter 6?

What practical steps can you take as you journey with God in your marriage?

Write a prayer to God about *serving God and others*.

Chapter 7

Victory at Last !

"And this is the victory that has overcome the world – our **faith**" (I John 5:4). Our assurance of victory is also found in Romans 8:31, "What then shall we say to these things? If God is for us, who can be against us?"

My husband does attend church fairly regularly and acknowledges God in many situations and conversations. He knows God exists. But I am praying for and looking for a "**true conversion**" experience. In John 20:24-29, Jesus appeared to the disciples after His resurrection. However, Thomas was not in the room with them. The following verses describe the event: "But Thomas, called Didymus, one of the twelve, was not with them when Jesus came. The other disciples therefore said to him, "We have seen the Lord." But he said to them, "Unless I see in His hands the print of the nails, and put my finger into the print of the nails, and put my hand into His side, I will not believe." "And after eight days His disciples were again inside, and Thomas with them. Jesus came, the doors being shut, and stood in the midst, and said, "Peace to you!" Then He said to Thomas, "Reach your finger here, and look at My hands; and reach your hand *here*, and put *it* into My side. Do not be unbelieving, but believing." And Thomas answered and said to Him, "My Lord and my God!" Jesus said to him, "Thomas, because you have seen Me, you have believed. **Blessed are those who have not seen and yet have believed.**"

My husband needs to have that ***personal revelation*** of Jesus where there is no doubt that He is real! When he has a profession of faith that rivals that of Thomas in scripture, that will be a day of celebration in heaven and on earth. His eternal salvation will be secured and his ***head knowledge*** will be replaced with ***heart knowledge*** in Jesus. Romans 10:20 is my husband's verse: "I was found by those who did not seek Me; I was manifest to those who did not ask for Me."

As this chapter literally unfolds before our eyes, let us continue in steadfast belief that God will perform what He promises! My husband's salvation is **sure**, as sure as God's faithfulness. "Let us hold fast the confession of our hope without wavering, for He who promised is **faithful**" (Hebrews 10:23).

To God be all the Glory!

 *Seek and Find*

1. In John 20:29 Jesus says, "Thomas, because you have seen Me, you have believed. Blessed are those who have not seen and yet have believed." Thomas insisted on seeing the Lord himself, when he learned he had missed Jesus' visitation with the other disciples. Read I Peter 1:8. How does Peter state our reaction to loving Jesus, but not seeing Jesus (in the natural)? What point does Paul make in II Corinthians 4:18? According to Hebrews 11:1, for what have we "hoped for" through Jesus? If salvation is our eternal reward, then what do we do with the saying, "seeing is believing"? Does that contradict what scripture teaches about faith? Why or why not?

2. Another example of believing without seeing is in the book of II Kings. Read II Kings 5:1-12. Naaman was the Captain of the army of Syria, yet he sought out help with his leprosy from the King of Israel. When the prophet Elisha heard of his plight, he asked the King to send him to his house. Naaman then proceeded to Elisha's house and stood outside expecting a grand reception. Why was Naaman so outraged over Elisha's instructions? Did he need to see Elisha face to face to receive a miracle from God? What wisdom was shared with Naaman by his servants regarding Elisha's request in verse 13? How is Naaman's attitude similar to that of Thomas in the book of John? How did both men glorify God in the midst of their humbling experiences?

3. Read Acts 9:1-8. Why is Saul's experience with the risen Lord Jesus different than that of Thomas in John 20? Do you think God suddenly and dramatically descended upon Paul in order to get his attention? How would his extensive religious background keep him from "seeing" the truth about Jesus? In verse 5 Saul (Paul) calls out "Who are You Lord?" Saul recognizes Him as "master", but not as LORD. When Jesus speaks to him, Saul's reaction is "trembling and astonishment." In Saul's case, "seeing is believing." How did Paul's experience prepare him for his ministry as one of the New Testament's greatest contributors? Was his conversion real? How do we know? In I Timothy 1:12-17, Paul shares his own testimony with Timothy about his conversion and ministry. How does he give glory to God for the unseen "intervention", that became so personal to him, on the road to Damascus?

4. As we wait for God's promise to us regarding our marriage, how does He expect us to act? What does Psalm 27:13-14 say about trust, faith, and waiting? Read Romans 5:5. What does Paul say about hope? To what does Paul compare our hope to in Hebrews 6:19? While we wait, we often waiver and lose our stamina to continue in our struggle. What does Isaiah say to us in Isaiah 40 verses 29 and 31? Endurance is key to holding onto the hope as time goes on. Read Isaiah 41:10. What does God promise to do when we are exhausted? Knowing what God's "right hand" represents, how does it make you feel, to know that He upholds us by His strength? Will it ever fail? What did Jesus tell Paul, according to II Corinthians 12:9 about His strength and our weakness? What does Paul say in Philippians 4:13?

How has God spoken to you through Chapter 7?

What practical steps can you take as you journey with God in your marriage?

Write a prayer to God about *your belief in God and who He is*.

EPILOGUE

As of the date of this book's publication, much has occurred. My husband has been through a metamorphosis with a supernatural alteration of his spirit man taking place right before my eyes. We don't always recognize the subtle changes taking place, but God knows what has transpired in the heart.

My husband often displays the love and grace of God in his everyday life, as he handles little crises and challenges with his elderly mother, our son and his future entry in the U.S. Marine Corps, or me and my mid-life changes. God has surely gifted this wonderful man with strength, love, and humility with his family.

I believe God will complete the work He has begun in my husband. With the Lord, a day is as a thousand years, and I know He can do above and beyond what we imagine – all for His glory. There will be growing and stretching ahead for both of us and as a married couple. We will give and take, and we will ebb and flow. God's plan is to bring unity to our marriage and fulfill our destiny in Christ together. **So be it**...

Thank you Lord, that You are drawing our husbands unto Yourself. Give them a desire to know You more fully. Cause them to rise up and take on the spiritual responsibility You have given them. May we, as their wives, respect them and bring them honor. May we be the helpmeet You have created us to be. We ask Your blessing on our marriages and give You all the glory and honor that is due. We ask this believing, and in the name of Jesus. Amen.

ABOUT THE AUTHOR

Author D.L. McCarragher began her journey of creative writing soon after coming to know Jesus as her personal savior. She enjoys using her spiritual gifts of encouragement and teaching in her home church. Her love of the Holy scripture and bible study are evident in her poetry and literary works. She and her husband attend Hibernia Baptist Church in Green Cove Springs, and reside in Fleming Island, Florida.

You may contact the author at:

ALABASTER BOX
PUBLISHING

www.Godmissionpossible.com

or email testimonials to:

deb@alabasterboxpublishing.com